# Transferring the Vision:

## Dynamics of Mentoring, Training and Teaching

By Stan E. DeKoven, Ph.D.

*Stan E. DeKoven, Ph.D.*

# TRANSFERRING THE VISION:
## Dynamics of Mentoring, Training and Teaching

Copyright (c) 2005 by Stan E. DeKoven

Vision Publishing Services

ISBN: 1-931178-44-5

All scripture quotations taken from the New American Standard Version of the Bible

Published by:

Vision Publishing
1115 D Street
Ramona, CA 92065
www.visionpublishingservices.com

## Acknowledgments

I want to give special thanks to our students around the world who are studying diligently, and achieving greatness in the Kingdom of God. Further, to our leaders of these centers of training and education in various regions of the world, the unsung heroes of our ministry, thanks for your faithful and effective service for our King. To Dr. Steve Mills, a partner in the training of men in the nations, a true servant, who introduced me to the teaching material from which this book is adapted, my humble thanks. Finally, to our staff in California who has worked behind the scenes to ensure that our centers and independent students have what they need to fulfill their purposes. Thanks to all of you for standing with the Vision of Vision.

*Stan E. DeKoven, Ph.D.*

# Table of Contents

Introduction ........................................................ 7

Chapter 1
    Understanding Leadership Training ..... 17

Chapter 2
    Goals of Learning ................................ 23

Chapter 3
    Helping Students Grow ....................... 31

Chapter 4
    Facilitating Learning ........................... 41

Chapter 5
    Methodology ....................................... 49

Chapter 6
    Increasing Learning Skills ................... 57

Chapter 7
    Techniques to Increase Learning ......... 65

Chapter 8
    Making the Class Come Alive ............ 71

Conclusion ........................................................ 77

*Stan E. DeKoven, Ph.D.*

## Introduction

**VISION OF VISION**

As with every great endeavor, whether in the natural world or God's spiritual Kingdom, there are many circumstances, events, conflicts and influences which determine the effectiveness of an endeavor.

Historically, triumphs came within the context of history, where generally common men and women were thrust to the forefront, and rose to the challenge at hand. Without the evil Pharaoh, would a Moses have been required? Without Saul's turning away from God, David's triumph would not have been needed. Without Israel's apostasy and subsequent captivity, Daniel and the three Hebrew children may not have had such monumental influence, and Ezra and Nehemiah would not have had walls to rebuild and revival fires to flame. Even in modem history, without the evil empire of Hitler, would Roosevelt, DeGaulle and Churchhill, let alone Bradley, Eisenhower and Patton have become admirable heroes in spite of their human weakness.

All of history and every truly significant ministry have come into being as with Esther, "for such a time as this." All of the human vessels that God has used throughout history have been imperfect, yet God in

His mercy and grace chooses whom ever He will to fulfill His purpose. He has always done things according to the counsel of His own will, and always shall.

Throughout the world, both in the world and the Church, there is a cry for leadership. A deep yearning exists for men and women of moral integrity and sincere desire to help God's chosen people to arise with a fresh vision for the future. Unsatisfied with the status quo, men and women are anxiously awaiting for true leaders who can bring them a sense of meaning, purpose and hope. For such a time as this is the call for visionary leaders, who will dedicate themselves to the task of world transformation. These leaders must be identified and trained to achieve Kingdom greatness.

Jesus Christ was born into the world during a similar time as ours. The Roman Government, with their ideology and idolatry were dominating the known world. God's chosen people were languishing in Palestine, oppressed and powerless. Their glorious past was all but forgotten under the oppressive hand of the Romans.

One would think the Hebrews would be somewhat used to their lot. Throughout their history, as with the history of the New Testament Church, their fate seemed to rise and fall in direct proportion to the

*Transferring the Vision*

obedience and vision (or lack thereof) of their leaders. When the leaders obeyed the Word of the Lord and followed righteousness, all was well. Ultimately, prosperity became their portion. When they walked in disobedience and rebellion, captivity, bondage and a lack of power or fulfillment became their lot.

As it has been said, there is nothing new under the sun. As we also observe in history, God is gracious and plenteous in mercy. God has never forgotten His covenant with the people of Abraham, Isaac and Jacob, or those grafted into the covenant by the blood of His precious Son Jesus. God has always provided a Moses, Gideon, Deborah, David, Hezekiah, Nehemiah, Ezra, Jesus, Luther or Wesley. Modern history provides us with ample examples of faithful men and women, filled with the power of God, who have provided a message and model of hope to each subsequent generation.

As we observe the signs of our times, it becomes only too apparent that we are in need of deliverance and guidance, which will come through visionary leaders equipped and released in this generation.

## WHERE TO LOOK, WHO TO SEEK

Some would look outside of the Church for such leadership. Many would look to political power, or attempt to lead through building a financial empire. Ultimately, God will raise up leaders in this generation who have His heart and His vision, and will in an uncompromising fashion lead the people of God as we prepare for the coming of the Lord.

Other Christians long for a great spiritual father. We should remember and give honor to those who have provided a foundation for us to build upon. However, in this final (we hope) outpouring of God's Holy Spirit, it will not be one or a few, but thousands and tens of thousands of common men and women who will know their God, display strength and take action (Daniel 11:32, NAS). It is the time for the Joshua generation to emerge and take their place in the harvest field, which is the Kingdom of God.

## THE EVERLASTIING VISION

Jesus told His disciples to make disciples of all nations. This would occur through identification (salvation/baptism) with Christ and through teaching them all that Jesus commanded (Matt. 28:18-20, Luke 24:27). The primary vision of Vision is to provide the resources necessary to effectively teach, equip, and restore those who through identification with the death, burial and resurrection of Christ are destined for service in God's Kingdom. Every believer in every nation must go beyond simple (yet profound) identification to full discipleship, maturity

*Transferring the Vision*

and wholeness in Christ, and thus compassionately live out their life in humble submission to Christ and His Word.

The vision, given to us by the Lord through His progressive revelation includes the following.

## THE THREE LEGS

First, the local Church, meaning the church within the city or locality, is the central place where the purposes of God are fulfilled. The Church/Ministry was not an after thought of God, but has been His will from the beginning. The Church today is the laboratory for the equipping/restoring of God's people. It is thus the central leg of God's Holy tripod. For a tripod (three threaded cord, etc.) to be strong, it must have its other legs.

The second leg is the Healing or Restoration Center. The Church, like a hospital, must be prepared to repair and rebuild the broken lives that enter her. When men and women are saved out of darkness they bring their deeds of darkness, often hidden in their hearts, into the Church. The results of the work of the devil in the lives of people, the impact of a sin tainted environment causes damage to the soul and body that needs loving care and appropriate medicine. This can include counseling, practical guidance, group support, and loving biblical confrontation, which over time will produce results that are lasting.

The third leg, the mirror of leg two is that of equipping or training. Every Church should be a worship center, every Church should be a healing center and every Church should be an equipping center, where believers can be systematically trained according to biblical pattern (see Acts 2:42; 11:19-26; 19:8-11). This training or education must be systematic, anointed, academic, and filled with life.

The Vision of Vision is to provide to the Body of Christ assistance, support, encouragement and resources to strengthen all three legs, and thus facilitate the preparation of the Bride of Christ for the Bridegroom (Rev. 19:7).

## THE PURPOSE OF THIS BOOK

About 6 years ago a prophet from South Africa prophesied into my life the need to train trainers, to equip equippers, to teach teachers how to teach more effectively, within the setting they may find themselves. Our materials, developed by some of the most outstanding Conservative Charismatic teachers in the world, were/are excellent. However, the best material requires the best possible instructor. We have felt for a long time that we are responsible to teach how to teach with the passion we carry as leaders of Vision. This book[1] is designed to be a first step in developing more effective teachers of the Vision material to fulfill the vision of training leaders for the next generation.

## THE PROBLEM

Most solutions begin with a problem. The problem we faced, and one commonly seen around the world, is the need to have qualified instructors to communicate the truths of God's word in a systematic and dynamic fashion. We (Vision) had already embarked upon the solution for much of the bigger problem, the need for men and women to be trained for the Harvest field. The solution to the problem of the church's need for leaders in all walks of life seems to be training of the Local congregation, and developing leaders in particular to fulfill the ministry for which God has gifted them. Education cannot replace the gifts of the Spirit, but rather helps the gifted person to develop and utilize their gifts.

The philosophy, goals, objectives and methods of any Church based training program must be based solely on the word of God. Paul the Apostle in Ephesians 4:7-13 states

---

[1] The author is grateful for the opportunity to adapt and expanded on the TEE Facilitators Manual by Lighthouse Outreaches, Directed by Dr. Steven Mills.

"But to each one of us grace was given according to the measure of Christ's gifts."

8 Therefore it says,

"WHEN HE ASCENDED ON HIGH,

HE LED CAPTIVE A HOST OF CAPTIVES,

AND HE GAVE GIFTS TO MEN."

9 (Now this *expression*, "He ascended," what does it mean except that He also had descended into the lower parts of the earth?

10 He who descended is Himself also He who ascended far above all the heavens, so that He might fill all things). 11 And He gave some *as* apostles, and some *as* prophets, and some *as* evangelists, and some *as* pastors and teachers, 12 for the equipping of the saints for the work of service, to the building up of the body of Christ; 13 until all attain to the unity of the faith, and of the knowledge of the Son of God to a mature man, to the measure of the stature, which belongs to the fullness of Christ.

Understanding the principles found in this passage is essential to our understanding of what is needed and what our ultimate goal is. In summary, Paul states that each member of the Body of Christ is gifted, with abilities that are needed for others in the church and beyond. Further, God has not only given the gifts but the gifted persons to minister in the body. The purpose of these gifted people is to restore the wounded, and equip or prepare other members of the church to serve in a large variety of capacities. The results of this will be the maturing of the church to fulfill its purpose in the earth. Thus, the specific result of teaching ministry will be people prepared who are then able to build up the church at large, and reach out in love to the community as a whole. This church will be filled with people who know who they are, what they believe and will be unified in purpose, having mature believers with knowledge of Christ and his word. This restoration, preparation, training, development and growth in Christ and his principles is not complete until all members come into the stature of the fullness of Christ, or maturity.

Therefore, the goal of our transformation through teaching is to see every member of the Body of Christ grow up, to become everything God wants us to be, so we can do all God wants us to do and continue to grow in Him and fulfill our purpose. This will only happen as men and women come to the knowledge of their gifts and callings, and are prepared through effective teaching and impartational learning, through the interaction between students and mentor...true Spirit led discipleship. Our hope is that through the teaching of Vision courses around the world, it will lead to mature men and women coming into the fullness of their purpose. We stand in hope, knowing it is the will of our Father for His "Kingdom to com and will to be done, on earth as it is in heaven."

# Chapter 1

# Understanding Leadership Training

Having been a teacher of the word of God for many years, I wonder sometimes if another book or booklet on teaching is really needed. Most people who read a book like this are already committed, have taught Sunday school or in other settings for many years. Yet, in all my studies, I never seem satisfied with my output. I always want to communicate better with my students the truths I am learning from my rich and consummate study of God's precious word. Perhaps you have a similar desire? If so, you already have a basic ingredient to becoming a training leader. We are never there, we are always learning, we always strive for more.

To be an effective trainer of trainers requires many skills, and begins with a clear and comprehensive philosophy of teaching and training, based upon principles of effective presentation.

## The Correct Worldview

To be an effective teacher/trainer, one must have a clear philosophy of what and why we do what we do. A philosophy, or worldview is the basic idea and purpose of anything a person tries to accomplish. For example, a pastor preaches to change the faith and life of a group of people, to help people to change, to inspire growth, etc. Everything a pastor does (or at least should do) will be determined by their world view, or desire to accomplish the purpose originally stated. There are a number of principles that will be the basis of our material taught as well as the method of teaching. First we must remember that

- All teaching must conform to Bible teachings and models. In 2 Peter 1:3 we are told that "His divine power has given us everything we need for life and godliness through our knowledge of him who has called us by his own glory and goodness."

The fact is, all teaching begins with a worldview. We choose to accept the revelation found in the Bible as the final definitive word for our Christian life. Thus, as a teacher of the world of God one must determine what philosophy or worldview will be used in developing your teaching ministry, or in essence one must ask themselves "what is the meaning and purpose of life and how does it affect what I am and do?"

Paul the apostle recognized the importance of "knowing". Paul uses the term "to know" in one form or another 70 times in his letters. Paul, however, warns us that knowledge can cause pride, that love is the key motivator for all we are to do; love for God and love for our neighbors. (1 Cor. 8:1). The parable of Jesus where he presents the wise and foolish man illustrates the folly of knowing without doing. (Luke 6:46) He also gave the commandment to "Go and make disciples of all nations, teaching them to obey all that I have commanded you." (Matt. 28:19, 20) But what did Jesus mean by teaching? In the original Greek text, the word to teach is the word Matheteuo, meaning to become a pupil, enroll as a scholar, disciple, instruct, teach. The style of teaching in those days was more like the old idea of an apprenticeship, or that of learning a trade. The purpose of learning was to do. Not only did the master tell the apprentice how to do the job, but he showed him by example, and then allowed the apprentice to try to do the work himself, under the master's supervision. The apprentice never became a master until he could do what the master could do. That is the goal of discipleship or of our teaching that the student will become like the master. From our perspective, a teacher has not really taught until the teaching has been caught by the disciple to such an extent that they can teach it also. In other words, for a teaching ministry to be effective, the student must have learned sufficiently to teach others (see 2 Tim. 2:2).

For teaching to be effective, what is learned must be practiced. Essentially, a disciple learns by hearing, observing and doing. Though many of us heard our parents say to us "do as I say, not as I do", the truth is, we do what we see. Jesus said, "Follow me." Paul said, "Be followers of me as I follow Christ." (1 Cor. 11:1) All there elements are needed for a teaching to be truly learned. It must be heard, it must be observed (a deeper level of looking, with the intent of gaining full understanding) and then it must be acted upon to become ones own.

As has been stated above, the goal of teaching is transformation, or change. In order for change to occur, a personal response to the teaching must be afforded. This process is readily seen in teaching children, who are curious to hear, observe and try any new thing until they get it. With adults, this is not always the case. Adults come to the learning experience with so much to offer. They have learned much by experience, both good and bad, but in the best sense they come to a learning experience with perspectives which can contribute to a richness of learning. One definition of teaching is "to cause to learn". With Adults, this is not always possible. As the old adage states, you can lead a horse to water, but you cannot make them drink is mostly true with adults. But equally true is that you can make them want to drink by pouring salt in their oats! Good teaching leads by facilitating or motivating the adult learner to want to learn, which is the art form of teaching adults. Thus, good teachers of adults are facilitators of the learning process. They are not necessarily course content experts, though expertise is obviously a blessing to have. More than that, by personality or technique, they are able to set the stage for students to want to learn as a part of their growth/change process. The teacher is not the source of knowledge, but can lead the student to discover knowledge from many sources. Jesus was the source; we only lead them to the source.

As an instructor, you might ask yourself the question, am I at the point in my life experience where I can share with others? Could I give the same offer to others that Paul did? (1 Cor. 11:1) Do I have all the knowledge I need or want, and does my life conform to what I already know (am I a good life example for others to follow). To be a facilitator, all you need is to be a bit ahead of those you are leading, so they can properly follow. In other words, you need to have the basic knowledge you are teaching ahead of your students it you are going to help them to follow a path to greater knowledge and understanding.

## A Final Observation

When I first attended University, especially in taking my course work in counseling, it always amazed me how dysfunctional many of the professors were. It seemed as though having neurotic symptoms, conflict with parents, unresolved hurts from the past were a necessary part of becoming a professor. Sadly, most of these professors were unable to do what they taught, but were intelligent enough to become highly paid and influential professors at prestigious universities. Though most of us can recall preachers and teachers in Christendom who have not lived what they preached, we know better than to follow them. It is essential, as a follower of Christ and teacher of God's word that we be more than hearers, but doers of the word also.

## Chapter 2

## Goals of Learning

In 2 Tim. 1:5, Paul, writing to his son in the Lord, Timothy, reminds him of the goal for instruction. This is the focus of our life as teachers. Paul states;

> "But the goal of our instruction is love from a pure heart, and a good conscience and a sincere faith."

It is obvious that Paul was a man with a goal in mind. He wanted to see transformation, a change from the inside out. So often in ministry we want to see an external change. We try to change the culture of a person, rather than affecting an inner transformation. Paul was clear. First, there had to be a change of affections (from self to Christ), a cleansed or purified heart was the most important goal (Love, which is from the word agape, meaning an unselfish affection, benevolence, such as from 1 John 4:20,21, to love God and love your brother), that flowed from a Pure heart (kardia/katharos, a clean heart, clear of past thoughts, feelings, from the center of self; blessed are the pure in heart, Matt. 5:8).

No mere ability to say the right words or to follow the leader would do. It was essential to Paul, and thus to Timothy and us that our first aim would be to see a person genuinely committed to Christ in their heart, as evidenced by a change of focus from self to Christ and others.

Secondly, as Paul taught the word of God, he expected to see a change in the thinking of the person. A good conscience is really a God conscience (from the Greek word suneidesis, meaning co-perception and a moral conscience, having the mind of Christ, 1 Cor. 2:16). The renewing of the mind (Rom. 2:1,2) comes as we hear the word and allow the word of God to transforming our thinking into the Lord's thoughts, also known as repentance. Repentance is not weeping, wailing and gnashing of teeth (Jesus called that the response of the lost in hell), though Godly sorrow does lead to repentance. Repentance is ultimately a change of thinking that leads to a change of lifestyle. Again, change is from the inside out.

Finally, Paul did want to see a change of behavior as well. A sincere faith was one which was spoken (anupokritos, sincere, without hypocrisy) faith, which is pistis in the Greek, means conviction, or an absolute reliance on Christ and his word, with an assurance that "all things work together for good to them that love God, and are called according to his purpose." (Rom. 8:28)

*Transferring the Vision*

**Practical Thoughts**

In a game of any kind, it is important to have the correct goal in mind. Nothing is more embarrassing to a player than to help out his opponents by putting a ball in the wrong goal. It is essential to know where and what your goal is, lest you do something in the wrong direction.

How often have we made the mistake of judging learning by knowing the rules of grammar or an algebraic formula? Even in Bible study we often think of a person as succeeding by how much scripture he/she knows, or how well they can argue a doctrine. In school we often make the examination the goal, rather than, as we have previously stated, the spiritual goals outlined by Paul the apostle.

So what are the goals of a leadership training program/course, and why do you really need goals?

One reason for goals is to be able to plan How to attain the goal we have chosen.

Therefore the objectives must be getting us nearer to the goal, or they are leading us farther away. The goal is the final judge of the value of objectives. Further, each course that is chosen, planned or taught must have a goal that contributes to attaining the goal of the course. In the school we could label the intermediate objectives the **course goals**, while the immediate objectives are the **lesson objectives**.

A good program is built like a house, one brick at a time. Each higher goal or objective rests squarely on those below. Below is a sample of a Goal and Objective for you to consider.

## Sample
## Goal and Objective

I. When the student is finished with this lesson he/she will be able to understand the meaning of Journey and Wholeness. <u>The goal of the student is to complete the reading of chapter 1 of the book *"Journey to Wholeness"* by Dr. Stan DeKoven, and develop a sermon outline on this chapter.</u>

    A. The objective is to complete the assignment presented above within one week, in proper format.
        1. The work is to be completed independently, and in typed format
           a. The student may ask for help from another student, but may not copy work, etc.

With a simple goal and objective as presented above, the student knows where he/she is going, and what is required of them to complete the task at hand.

*Transferring the Vision*

Again, why are goals needed? The goals of a program indicate the idea the church, school or administration has in mind for the students when they have successfully completed the program. When Nehemiah returned from Babylon to Jerusalem he had only one idea in mind, to rebuild the walls of the city. To the contrary, Ezra's only goal was to rebuild the temple. That is all they talked about or tried to motivate the people to accomplish. As a result, they accomplished their goals because they know what they wanted to do, stated clearly, and pursued only activities that lead to the goal intended. We must ask the question, do your students know what you are trying to accomplish? If not, why not? Were you clear in the statement of the goals and objectives?

The goal guides the student to plan his studies, homework, time, etc. How many times in a class have you wondered just what the teacher was trying to accomplish or what he wanted you to do? When the student is clear regarding what is required of them, they can cooperate in the learning experience more fully. It is a sad fact that many students get discouraged because they do not have a clear concept of what is wanted from the student to complete the course being taught. Adults, far more than children, must know where the teacher is leading the student. They have been determining their goals and paths for years, and do not want to waste their time on wrong turns. Thus, as a visionary teacher or course facilitator, you need a goal and plan to help the student remain on track. The immediate and intermediate objectives also give the student and teacher alike the ability to check the progress of the educational process. Without a good plan with good goals and objectives the educational process can get bogged down in a morass of detail of irrelevant material. We can easily get back on track by seeing if what is being presented is leading to the stated objective or goal.

Remember, a goal or objective will help measure progress or the accomplishment. This is the purpose of *evaluation*. That is why a target has circles on it, to see how close you can come to the center. Teaching with purpose helps the instructor to avoid such problems as incessant story telling or teaching/ preaching Christian clichés to fill time. Goals and objectives not only help the facilitator, but the students as well to see how they have grown, learned, changed, etc. It is impossible to evaluate without stated goals and objectives.

## A Good Goal or Objective

What makes a good goal or objective? First of all, it is necessary to put the goal or objective in writing. Though that sounds very simple, it is truly essential.

Secondly, the goal or objective must be clear enough for all to understand. Even if the student has no knowledge of the subject, he or she should at least be able to understand the purpose for the course or class being taken before entering the educational experience.

Third, the goal or objective must be observable for evaluation, that is, the words used to describe the result must say what the student can *do* when he/she has completed the assignment. Thus, the goal or objective must be clear, non-ambiguous, which can be interpreted in only one way. The conditions for satisfactorily completing the task must be defined in detail.

**Evaluation**

A primary reason for writing goals and objectives is to have a standard by which evaluation can be made. Essentially, objectives provide criteria for evaluation of the student. In a good evaluation, you will answer the questions; did the student attain the goal or objective? Did the facilitator/teacher do the necessary job of teaching the material sufficiently to ensure that the student could meet the criteria? Finally, did the lesson meet the stated goal, of preparing the student to fulfill what has been learned in practical terms?

When a goal or objective is clear, understandable, in writing, etc. it sets the stage for proper evaluation. Most students want to know how they did, and if they have missed the mark, why? If, as an instructor, you are able to take them to the objectives and demonstrate how they have not satisfied the goal or objective, you rarely hear a complaint. Most complaints in evaluation are really complaints about unclear or inadequate goals or objectives, not students who are incapable of completing the assignment.

## Chapter 3

## Helping Students Grow

One of the primary objectives of all mentoring, training and teaching is to assist a student to develop his or her ministerial skills, by helping the student develop his or her own goals through the learning process. As a mentor or facilitator, one must consider several points of logistics before launching a training center or ministry. These include:

- The school building itself, or where are you going to meet.
- Classroom space within the building
- Library facilities and books to fill the library
- Qualified professors to teach the courses
- Office space for administration
- Dormitory and dining space if that is a part of your program

There may be other items of importance to consider, such as transportation, etc., but this is a good beginning. If you chose any of the above items as important to starting your school, you need to consider what is more important than any of these…the students. Without students, there can be no school. Not only must you have students but the entire program, administration, building or courses, etc., cannot be planned until the student is considered. Everything else exists for the student, not the administration or the school.

Thus, it goes without saying that the school must be student oriented, and the student is our number one concern (after pleasing the Lord). As we have already pointed out in the last chapter, we are dealing with adults who by experience know who they are, what they want to do, when they want to do it, and how it should be done. They must be treated with respect, consulted, and considered in the development of the educational programs.

This is, most assuredly, different than our experience growing up. As children, all was chosen for us, and the convenience of the school and teachers, etc., was considered above the needs of the students. The student knew little or nothing about the educational process, and the teacher was the king or queen of the classroom. The teacher set the rules and the student did what he or she was told to do. There were no choices for the students.

With adult students, the best way to determine what will best facilitate the learning process for them is to ask them. Simple I know, but adults need to be consulted, not lectured to. With this in mind, there are several things that you as a teacher/mentor need to know before you can plan a training program. They include:

*Transferring the Vision*

- Where your students live?
- Where they work?
- Are they predominantly married or single?
- How long have they been saved and members or a local church?
- What have they done in the local church as far as service?
- What is their level of formal education? Informal? Life experience?
- What Bible training have they had before now?
- What is their income and ability to pay fees?

Once you have ascertained some of this information, you can begin to develop a workable profile of your "typical" student. This information will help you in planning your program. Your profile will become a descriptive, and very likely you will be able to discover several categories, as noted above.

With this information, you can then determine:

- When and where to hold classes
- How much you can charge for a course, thus what you can pay in honorariums, etc.
- How far they must travel
- How you present your teaching program
- How to set your goals and objectives to meet the needs of the students.

It is then possible to describe what the student wants to become, based upon the findings, the students' education and experience, etc. From there it is then possible to determine what a student needs to do to accomplish their stated goal. The mentor then can assist the student to develop their goals and objectives, and state in clear terms (and in writing) what learning courses, experiences, reading etc., need to be done to attain the goals and objectives stated.

It is then helpful to ask yourself the question, what are some of the things you need to know to prepare a training program? It is probably not possible to arrive at the final goal in one simple jump, but rather by advancing step by step through the immediate and intermediate objectives called courses.

Below is a diagram that can help us to understand the ideas involved. We will work through a simulated experience. This may sound a bit difficult and tedious as a facilitator, but even though you are not called upon to prepare or administer a program, your understanding as to how this process works will aid you in working within an educational system. To follow is a brief diagram illustrating what a teacher can use to develop individualized goals for a student.

*Transferring the Vision*

## PROSPECTIVE STUDENT
(1)
What he/she is?

_____

_____

_____

## DESIRED RESULT
(2)
What he/she must be able to do?

_____

_____

_____

## PROCESS
(3)
What is to be learned?

_____

_____

_____

In this diagram, list number one presents the student as he or she is. In the second diagram, you list what the student envisions themselves to be. List three provides the process necessary to achieve what the student wants, or to get them from 1-3. What are the specifics of the process of assisting a student to move from what he is to what he wants to be?

The process can consist of lessons, experiences, readings, seminars, on-line learning, etc. Even the student's ministerial experience such as Sunday school teaching, leading worship, etc. can be evaluated as a part of the process. It reality, anything that leads the student toward the goal for which they are aiming can be seen as a legitimate activity.

It was noted above, that the Student was the number one element in the process of learning. The second element is the Process itself. The third and final element in this learning process is the teacher, or as Jesus would have seen it, the discipler. This person can be called a teacher, facilitator, or mentor. As we think about this process, it is important to remember that Jesus never had a school building to work from, nor a program per se, let alone a staff or curriculum, but he did have a process that we can observe in scripture. He said in Matt. 10:25, "It is enough for the student to be like his teacher." If the student becomes like his facilitator, the mentor is obliged to be an example of what he is teaching. To lead, a person must be worthy of being followed. Remember the statement of Paul; "Imitate me as I imitate Christ." (1 Cor. 11:16)

To reiterate, the student is the most important element in the educational program. We then stated that we must discover what the student wants, and is capable of doing before planning a program. Once we can express what we see as the student's goal or objective, he then can read it to see if that is what he desires to accomplish. If it is, he is then ready to pursue that goal. If not, the goal can be adjusted. There is also the possibility that the student's goals are not the same as those of the institution. For example, if a student desires to receive a liberal arts education leading to an advanced degree from a graduate school in a liberal arts subject, they might be disappointed, especially if the school you teach in only offers theological courses, not liberal arts ones. The student could complete the theological program, expecting to go on to a graduate school, and not be allowed to do so. Thus, if the goal cannot be reached through your teaching program, the student should seek help elsewhere. It is essential to match the student with the proper teaching program, so the student and the school are in harmony, avoiding potential difficulties in the future.

Beyond the choice of goals there are other things to consider, such as the level of teaching. This will depend on both their education in formal schooling as well as their level of studies in Christian subjects. It would not be convenient to place a novice and mature Christian together any more than it would to mix $6^{th}$ graders with college students. However, once you have described the prospective students it is quite simple to form any number of classes to meet the varied needs and interests as well as to plan lessons according to their level of education. Thus, it is essential to begin the process at the level of the student, perhaps challenging them to perform higher than their present capability. No matter how interesting your subject may be to you, the mentor must resist the temptation to go far beyond your objective for that lesson. Allow the objective to be your guide and control.

There are four additional items to consider as a part of the educational process. The first is ***time***. Your questions should have revealed the time that the students have available to give to the learning process. Too often we have a time that is sacred to us for school. In one church the survey revealed that half could attend class on Saturday, while the other half could not. The half that could not attend on Tuesday evenings were able to attend on Saturday, while the Saturday people could not get out on Tuesday. With a situation like this, the solution can be difficult to some and obvious to others. To solve this problem the church offered two classes of 20 each, one on Saturday and the other on Tuesday. This is in keeping with the rule of thumb that the student is the most important element of the school.

Secondly, ***finances*** are an important element to consider. This includes how much to charge, and the students' ability to pay. Every ministry school wants to assist as many people as possible. Yet experience

*Transferring the Vision*

tells us that the concept of implied value is true also for Bible students...if it is free it is worth little or nothing. We want the students to value the education they are receiving, and yet do not want to make it too expensive, unaffordable to most. A balance with wisdom is needed.

Third, but to be discussed in greater detail in a later chapter, is the ***place*** the class is to be held. For maximum exposure to the school, it is location, location, location.

Finally, there are the ***instructional materials*** to be used in the course. This has been an area of grave concern to Vision, especially in light of our vision to take the whole Word to the whole world. This requires texts, study guides, exams, etc. For you as a facilitator, training and mentoring in the Vision system, this problem has been amply solved.

With all of these elements in place, the mentor is ready to teach with a high degree of confidence. As with all educational ministries of worth, the Vision program is continually being modified to meet the needs of students and teachers alike. Your feedback is vitally important to this process.

*Stan E. DeKoven, Ph.D.*

## Chapter 4

## Facilitating Learning

One of the important tasks to grasp as we approach mentoring, teaching and facilitating learning is to understand the difference between pedagogy and androgogy. Over the years, there has been much study done in the field of pedagogy. As the name implies, ("ped" comes from the Latin root meaning child, "gogy" to teach), thus pedagogy is all about the process and philosophy of teaching children. Many of the principles of teaching children have simply been altered to use in teaching adults, approaching adults as simply older children. However, there are significant differences between teaching children and adults, especially in the fast paced and technologically changing world we live in. Thus we must ask ourselves the question…

**What Factors Differ in Teaching Adults?**

First, pedagogy assumes that children have very little experience or knowledge of life to draw upon in the learning process. They are essentially a "blank slate" to be written upon by the teacher. The result of this is that the teacher is assumed to have the knowledge that will be transferred by any and all means to the student, providing experience for the student to build upon for further learning.

Secondly, the child is required to attend school by parents and later by society in general to be able to qualify for a job or placement in a University. Essentially, formal education is seen as a passport to success in our world (and in many ways, rightly so). The greater percentage of students we will work with in our ministry education are not there by compulsion, but voluntarily. They have chosen to learn for either personal reasons, to help others, or to prepare them to fulfill a call of God on their lives. Thus, they are learning by personal choice, not to please someone in authority over them.

Third, in pedagogy it is assumed that the teacher or the administration knows already what needs to be learned by the student, thus limited choices are afforded the students. The things to know are already fixed, and the students are only to do what they are told to do. The typical adult does not appreciate being told what he or she needs to learn because each one's life experience, natural abilities and interests are highly individual. They want to choose and direct their learning process, with the help of guidance from learned facilitators.

Now, though this is generally true about adults, in highly structured and hierarchical cultures, where authority is from the top down, this desire to choose is less evident, more subtle for fear of retribution. Thus the adult student may feign compliance. All adult students require choices, though in some

*Transferring the Vision*

cultures, limited logical choices are necessary in one's presentation of a course of instruction. It behooves us to remember that most adults have some negative memories of school days in the past. Being humiliated because you did not know an answer, studying math which you hated (especially for me, algebra, I always wondered if it the subject could be a demon!), having to comply with assignments that made little or no sense was the experience of too many of the students we will be working with. We must therefore recognize the unique needs and gifts of the average adult learner. There are several basic differences in adult and child education. They include:

| **Adult** | **Child** |
|---|---|
| • Problem centered | • Content centered |
| • Participating | • Non-participating |
| • Draw on past experience | • Little past to draw on |
| • Learning is learner oriented | • Learning is teacher/content centered |
| • Learner is active in planning | • Authority provides planning |
| • Evaluation is mutual | • Evaluation is authority oriented |
| • Evaluation directs new | • Evaluation classifies learner |

learning
- Learning is experiential
- Learning is a choice
- Learning is transmitted
- Learning is obligatory

In teaching children, the focus of the learning is content driven, not skill oriented. Both content and skill seemed to be important to Jesus in his teaching, as stated by Luke.

> "Indeed, O Theophilus, I made the first report concerning all things which Jesus began both to do and to teach." (Act 1:1)

Jesus, in his ministry, both taught (like with the sermon on the mountain, Matt. 5-7) and demonstrated. He cast out spirits, healed the sick, cared for the needy, encouraged the downtrodden, etc. Jesus taught and did, and adult learners benefit most from both types of learning, which is practically presented and freely chosen (Jesus chose his disciples, but they chose him as well).

Mathew 4:18 finds Jesus choosing mature men to teach. He did not choose teenagers or children, nor simply volunteers from the crowd. His first command was to follow me; the second was I will make you fishers of men.

*Transferring the Vision*

His command to follow him implies that Jesus was interested first and foremost in a relationship with his followers. In Mark 3:14 Jesus chose his disciples that they "might be with him." The relationship that Jesus called his disciples into required that they would hear what he would say and observe all that he would do. Through this relationship, a transformation would occur, where they would become essentially like him. Jesus is our model of teaching and training, but with a vast difference. On our best days as an instructor, we will never be the source or essence of life that Jesus was and is, nor can we assume that we can make changes in men and women supernaturally…only the Holy Spirit in cooperation with the person can make such a transformation. We are only facilitators of the process of change, though discipling is more than just the accumulation of knowledge; it is change. Christ does change us through the teaching process, in spite of the limited vessels he uses to accomplish his purpose.

Finally, Jesus told his disciples that the same works he did they would do also, and even greater ones. At least twice during the disciples' training period Jesus sent them out to do what he had been doing. Learning for these unsophisticated but willing adults was an experience learned, then practiced until proficient.

In dynamic teaching, the teacher and the learner should both participate in the learning process. Many times, in the midst of teaching or preaching, especially while interacting with students, the Lord will give an insight into scripture or a principle of the Word that I had not previously seen. These are precious moments, which are often shared in the dynamic interchange between teacher and student.

In instructing adults, a positive climate with reduced stress is needed. We should, based upon the resources we have, provide for physical comfort, adequate variety of teaching experience, and mobility. It is helpful if the learning space does not resemble a school room and the seating is not a throwback to an early childhood experience. As much as possible, a living room environment or a local shade tree can be the most conducive to a positive learning environment.

## Pre and Post Course Evaluations

One helpful, though not absolutely required, activity of teaching that can facilitate learning is to conduct pre and post evaluations. The precept "begin with the known and move to the unknown." applies even more in adult education. A teacher will need to determine the level of knowledge a student has in the subject matter you are teaching prior to commencing the teaching process. Pre-course evaluations can yield much information as to needs, interests, values, and previous knowledge and experience. If questions are asked regarding the course material to be presented the facilitator as well as the student can observe and evaluate where they are in relation to the subject matter. Each student will have his/her own level that must be considered. A vast difference will probably be found in desire, motivation, best learning modality, etc. If you cannot use their experience and ability in a positive manner, they may use it defensively.

Although the traditional examination or test may be abhorrent and to be avoided for the adult learner, there is a need for evaluation of what has been accomplished during the course. Tests have been used mainly to classify the student in relationship to what the teacher sees as good or in relationship to other students. The adult doesn't care as much about grades that compare one to the other as the younger learner might. He or she wants to know how much they have advanced or learned. The interest is more in how much they know rather than how much they don't know. Thus, evaluations should be relevant to the course content, and designed to give clear feedback to the student in regards to their progress towards completion of course goals. Further, post evaluations should go both ways. That is, the student should be properly evaluated, along with the teacher and course content itself. This process of evaluation is a healthy way to insure that the course's goals are met, the course is improved for the future, and that the needs of the students are satisfied.

Remember, learning is a verb, not a noun. It is a journey, not a destination. Thus, the designers of the highway and the drivers of the vehicles definitely need a consistent philosophy from which to operate. If the learners have helped choose and design the learning process, they are much more likely to pursue the goals with high motivation. Thus, preparation of the class and the student to learn is a key to the learning/teaching process.

# Chapter 5

# Methodology

It would have been wonderful to observe the teaching methods of Jesus...the true Master Teacher. Unfortunately, we are so far removed from the culture of the day, we can at best only approximate the teaching methods of Jesus. Further, as we are 2000 years farther ahead in technology than Jesus, we have many distinct advantages in our teaching that Jesus did not have. Without doubt, Jesus was the Master Teacher, and the apostle Paul sets a good example of following in his Master's pattern. We can extrapolate from the Word of God principles and patterns they followed that made them successful in their ministry, recognizing that the principles and patterns of that day are germane for our own.

The most important aspect of the method of teaching of Jesus and Paul was that it was highly relational. As teachers, both were intimately involved in the lives of those being taught. Thus, as facilitators of the learning process, we must also be personal in our relationship with our students. Just as a truck and trailer work together to accomplish the carrying of a load, so are a teacher and student to work together for the process of learning.

Jesus chose men and women who were to be with Him in His mission by divine foreknowledge. His purpose for choosing these was to transform them into His own image. For them to be taught, they had to be willing to submit to His authority, which probably caused little difficulty due to the authority with which Jesus taught. With this in mind, teachers should always be looking for men and women with a heart to learn, minds open to the Word of God, and willing to submit to the process of growth and change. Sadly, many leaders fill slots with bodies, rather than waiting on the Lord to provide the key ones with which to build. Jesus is still calling and transforming men into His likeness. He gives them His Spirit and the Holy Spirit in turn gives them the gifts of the Spirit. He then gives them to the Body of Christ to minister.

Remember, Paul told Timothy, his true son in the Lord, to choose faithful men that would be able to teach others also. We as leaders and facilitators of the learning process must learn to recognize the gifted persons in the Body and call them to become servants in the church.

Jesus took imperfect men, taught them for 3 plus years, and even when He had completed the School of the Messiah they still did not fully understand His teachings or His mission (see Acts 1). Imperfect though they were, He had trained them to be disciples (learners), and they continued to grow in the grace of

God. We cannot expect to perfect our disciples but we can get them headed in the right direction, by the grace of God and our diligent and patient teaching.

The second method of training was that it was accomplished (for the most part) in a group. A person can certainly study the Bible at home, and they should. Correspondence study is an effective method of learning, as is video or internet training, if that is all that is available. However, the preferred method of instruction is in a small group, with opportunity for dialog, not just lectures. It is true that teaching a small group was a faster way for Jesus to duplicate His ministry, but the main reason for the group process is that the church is a body, a body in which each member depends upon the other. Learning from the Master is one thing, but learning from and how to work with each other is entirely another. Through group interaction and group problem solving, iron sharpens iron, and we learn to grow together to fulfill God's purposes.

The third method is applied learning. Biblical truths are not an abstraction. They are practical and to be practiced. Jesus was always careful to point out differences between what a person professed to believe and what he did. Remember the hypocritical Pharisees? They often professed one thing but did another. Applied learning is what the teaching of Jesus was all about in relation to sending his disciples out for ministry (see Matt. 10:1-8). Jesus gave them specific instructions regarding the continuation of the ministry of Christ.

Based upon the authority of Christ, and having acted upon his authority, the disciples experienced similar results as did Jesus. In II Peter 1:16, Peter states that they didn't "follow cleverly invented stories…but we were eyewitness of his majesty." Jesus told his disciples, "Freely you have received, freely give." Jesus practiced practical faith or faith in practice.

One goal of an effective teaching ministry is to bring the practical into the classroom. This is an art form, requiring creativity and imagination. With prayerful effort, the practical aspects of ministry can be developed in almost every class taught.

The fourth method of learning can be coined auto learning. That is, the ability for an individual student to learn on their own, or at least outside of a formal classroom setting. Auto learning can include such activities as directed learning from a book or perhaps self-directed learning in an individual project.

## Paul's Perspective

Evidently Paul thought Jesus' method was more than adequate, for he followed His example. As can be readily seen in Paul's instruction to Timothy, he was concerned that he (Timothy) follow the pattern that

Paul had learned and had subsequently imparted to Timothy.

> "And the things which you have heard from me in the presence of many witnesses, these entrust to faithful men, who will be able to teach others also." (2 Tim. 2:2)

Paul began his ministry by personally training others. He chose young men such as John- Mark, Timothy, Titus, and many others to follow him as he followed Christ. He taught them, both in word and especially in action, as an example for them to follow. In the process he no doubt gave them ample opportunity to practice what they had heard and observed in him.

This raises the question, which of these principles are we using in our leadership training in the average local church? Further, which do we need to begin or do more, if we are going to see a new generation of faithful men and women raised up to serve the church and the community?

## A Traditional Learning Method

Many people will attend a class or seminar, sit down in what we hope is a comfortable chair in a room with comfortable temperature and lighting, and wait to be taught. This type of learning provides for mass information in a relatively short period of time, but rarely satisfies the adult learner. This method has been called "storehouse filling." The teacher has a quantity of knowledge that must be poured into the empty and open head of the learner. Technically this is called transference of knowledge, and has a place in the overall educational process.

However, as we have previously noted, adults need and want to participate in the learning process. Finding ways to engage the adult learner in the process of learning is vital to the successful outcome of the process. There are several ways to engage an adult in the process of learning, which include:

- Reading and preparing material for lessons before the class, which will increase the amount of learning exponentially.
- Providing opportunity for dialog, questions, and general interaction with the instructor is a helpful way to increase learning. Of course, one must be cautious with the overall dynamics of the teaching process, and some students may want to "hide" and others "dominate." But when questions and dialog are well managed in a group setting it is an excellent way to learn.
- Giving practical assignments, from roll-playing to skits to dramas to leading a part of the teaching can help pique interest and engage the student in the learning process. We are only limited by our imagination, and the cultural restraints that must be considered.

*Transferring the Vision*

We must remember that if the student waits to hear the teacher give an answer, less than 12% of the information will be retained. If the student can see the answer visually (thus the reason such tools as PowerPoint are so potentially helpful), you will retain another 55%, but if the student has read and interacted with the lesson material on their own, they will retain the maximum amount of learning. This is the biblical process presented in scripture. Let us remember that:

- Jesus taught them orally.
- Jesus demonstrated what he taught, so His disciples might see the teaching.
- Jesus had them do what they had learned, or follow the pattern of Christ in His ministry.

Every time a student encounters truth, and interacts with it, that truth is reinforced for the student, deepening what has been learned. In the teaching methodology of Vision all instructors must endeavor to employ these insights. In the process of training, mentoring and teaching, facilitators will seek to impart information from both the teaching/facilitating and the required study materials. A well trained facilitator will be an example of that which is being taught. If one is teaching soul winning, the instructor should have some fresh results of their own to share. All instruction of adults must find ways to assist students to practice what they have learned. Thus, in the average adult class, opportunity for the teaching of fellow students should be facilitated at certain stages in the learning process. Of course, in class it is safe, primarily a simulation of the real teaching environment. A student's real experience will come when they begin to teach their own class, which is the hope of every School of Ministry, that students will become the faithful ones who are able to teach others also. The students' greatest learning will take place as they DO what they have learned.

## Chapter 6

## Increasing Learning Skills

Before moving forward to determine how we can best assist students to increase their leaning skills, it is judicious for us to look back to our first principle, "The student is the most important element in the learning process."

In previous chapters, we have likened the student to an apprentice (disciple). Further, we have stressed the importance of developing the whole person, body, soul and spirit. We have also delineated that knowing should lead to a change in the person; that is, their very being is changed through an encounter with the dynamic truth of God's word. The result of change should include that of a different attitude and a different comportment; their lifestyle should be demonstrably changed through the teaching/learning process.

We should remember from our first chapter the importance Paul places on "to know" or "knowing," He (Paul) further emphasizes that he did not "want you to be ignorant"; he wanted or expected change to occur through the mentoring/training dynamic. Our question is, how can we be sure that the student is really learning what is being taught? How can we know if we have presented too much material to be properly digested, or not enough to challenge our students to further study?

One tool that is effectively used to determine progress in learning is to provide periodic quizzes and tests. They are a 'short cut' way to tell what is happening with the student. This will provide some quick information to us on the effectiveness of our teaching, but it does not achieve the overall goal. We must be cautious here. Too often we are satisfied with a repeating of a scripture verse without understanding or a repeating of a doctrine verbatim without understanding its meaning or application.

We have presented a four-step process to effective learning. All four steps are important in the learning process, if it is to be life transforming for the students. The steps are:

- Knowing
- Teaching
- Being
- Doing

Knowledge is the key to the change process. Keep in mind that knowing, especially simple facts and figures, is not an end in itself. The fact is, being should change what a person does. Finally, the act of doing should enliven a fresh desire to learn even more; and so the cycle continues. Thus, facilitators of

*Transferring the Vision*

the learning process are to create an ongoing, continuing, learning-growing process.

As a writer and teacher, I am often called upon to teach the same subject in various locations over and over again. Many have asked me how I keep the teaching from growing stale, my enthusiasm from waning. The only way is to remain vibrant in our personal relationship with Jesus, and to be a forever learner. The facilitator must also be a learner! Every time you facilitate a course, you should become a closer likeness to Christ, hunger to know Him better, and become a better doer of the Word and a better communicator of truth. As you teach, the Lord in His grace will bring fresh revelation of His word and purpose. The fact is, I have never preached the same message twice nor taught the same lesson twice. It is always fresh, if you are always learning and growing in Christ.

Too many teachers hide behind a stack of ancient notes and lecture the same material year after year. Every class should be a growing experience. Because you are a learner, you cannot only know but must also experience these seven laws of learning.

## The Seven Laws of Learning

These Seven Laws are helpful to us as we teach for greater effectiveness. They are not immutable, but a guideline for our benefit. Each is reviewed here briefly.

1. ***Start where the student is*** and lead him where he wants to go. Another way of stating this is, start with what the student knows and lead her to what she needs to know.

To facilitate this process, questions must be asked. The simplest and the least assuming are to ask the student what he or she wants from the class. For example, if a blind man wanted you to help him go someplace, what is the first thing you must do? You must ask him where he wants to go. Secondly, you must then be willing to engage the blind man (student) where they presently are, and with agreement lead them to where they want to be. To lead a person requires relationship, which requires a certain level of trust as you work together to accomplish the learning goal.

Essentially, the facilitator is to work toward forming an intimate relationship with the student. The facilitator must know the student, care for the student, and help the student move toward his/her goals. He must know what the student already knows and has experience to be able to build on his past knowledge.

Jesus did this when he used parables from the everyday life of the fisherman, the farmer, the herdsman, etc. He spoke about taxes, sacrifices, marriage, food, water, light and death. These were all things the students had experienced and could easily relate to.

2. The second principle or law of learning is a corollary to the first: ***Teach line upon line.***

As you would build a building of bricks from the bottom up, so build upon what you have already taught. It is never wise to assume the student knows a certain amount of material. Check his present knowledge to see where to start. Build on a solid foundation, and then add additional knowledge to that strong foundation (remember, our foundation is Christ.).

3. ***Teach what the student wants to learn***, appeal to his/her interests.

We all have our own interests we would like to teach, but you will soon lose your students if you do not teach to their interests. Not many students today are interested in Shakespearean quotes, historical illustrations, or technical details. The Haitians say, "Put the medicine where it hurts," or some others say, "Don't scratch where it doesn't itch." Again you must know the students to be able to apply the medicine in the right place. Of course, as an educator, you will always try to lift the level of your students by teaching just a bit above their perceived abilities, and motivate them to reach to higher heights for the Lord.

### 4. *Encourage the student to learn.*

A trainer must be able to challenge a student to learn; you must excite them. Since enthusiasm is more caught than taught, it helps for you to be excited yourself. It has been a joy to see formerly fearful or easily distracted and discouraged students become excited about subjects they had previously avoided (like church history or hermeneutics). Of course, somehow the student must see that this area of learning is going to benefit him/her. Motivating students is a never-ending responsibility.

### 5. *Involve the student in learning through group discussion.*

When a student participates:

- You are learning about the student.
- She is expressing herself orally, thus reinforcing learning.
- You can evaluate what is actually taking place in the learning process.
- The students share with one another from their knowledge and experience.
- This gives the student a sense of being appreciated and understood.

- This clarifies ambiguous thinking, and facilitates deeper learning.

Frequently in the teaching of Jesus, he engaged his disciples in questions, challenged their thinking, and facilitated discussion (Who do you say the Son of Man is?). These discussions often lead to the discovery of new insights, or what we often call revelation (You are the Christ, the Son of the Living God!). We also see in the letters of Paul implied dialog, as he answered questions posed to him from the churches he gave oversight to.

Discussion is created and stimulated by good questions. We will study how to use poignant questions later.

6. ***Reinforce every important idea or concept.***

Telling, lecturing, reading, hearing, studying, reciting, etc. do not constitute learning. They may be a part, but are not the whole. Reinforcing does not mean repeating the same thing several times, but rather returning to the same concept and presenting it in different ways. Read it, say it, see it, illustrate it, do it, write it.

7. ***For learning to occur, the student must put what is learned into practice.***

We have already discussed the futility of knowing without doing. Not only is it a waste of both instructor and student time, it is incomplete learning, especially in terms of the goal of discipleship-apprenticeship. A student may be able to answer all the questions about how to swim, and describe how to swim in excellent prose, but until they can get in the water and swim, they do not know their subject. An apprentice mechanic may be able to tell you how to fix a car, but until he can make it run well, he has not learned his trade. The school and the facilitator must devise ways for the students to practice what they learn.

A facilitator of learning is looking to fulfill the goals of each of these laws through the teaching process. As with anything, the rules may seem cumbersome when you first attempt to follow them, but become natural as you practice them in your teaching process.

## Chapter 7

## Techniques for Facilitating Learning

When considering techniques, it is essential to be able to describe various techniques used in teaching with their relationship to the methodology discussed in Chapter 5. Along with this, the facilitator will need to know how to evaluate various methods and their effectiveness in learning and bringing about change in the lives of the students.

**Techniques of Teaching**

There are several important techniques that need to be learned to be effective in the teaching of students. They include:

- **Lecture**

In principle this denotes simple oral-verbal communication of material spoken by the teacher. This can be both boring and leave the learner passive, unless the lecturer is a fascinating speaker. Most speakers believe they are just that, unique and fascinating, but in truth very few qualify. I am privileged to have sat under two very dynamic lecturers, Dr. Joseph Bohac and Dr. Ken Chant, and have suffered through innumerable bores that shall remain nameless for the sake of mercy. Of course, a lecture can be spiced up with juicy illustrations, stories, colorful language, etc., but it takes a truly gifted man or woman to hold an audience for any length of time (beyond 30 minutes for most adults).

Lecture is the traditional student-teacher relationship from the dark ages and the beginning of higher education as a separate discipline. Lecture provides a bit of emotional security for the teacher and demands the least in immediate preparation. The belief of many lecturers is, if it is true and good why change it each year?

Though the lecture method is widely used in seminary and Bible college settings (and most Sunday morning messages) the lecture method provides for limited student participation. Lecture provides an efficient way of delivering large amounts of material in a relatively short period of time if that is the goal. Unfortunately, lecture by itself, even when supplemented with numerous aids and illustrations, produces limited life change. Even though a person may answer all test questions correctly, if they have not changed in attitudes and actions, time and energy has been wasted.

- **Supplemented Lecture**

This has become very popular and far more effective than lecture alone. Things used to supplement a lecture can include visual aids (such as PowerPoint if available) to illustrate the lesson, the asking of comments at the end of a lecture or the asking of a few questions to see if anyone happens to be listening. A syllabus or a handout to follow the lecture also helps the student to track the content of the presentation and adds another dimension to the class.

- **Reading Assignments**

One thing that can be done to enhance the learning process is to assign Pre-class reading. This activity alone increases participation in class, and assists the student in preparation for dialog on the subject being studied. The class then reinforces and clarifies the reading assignment. Reading after the class has little impact, though completing assignments related to the subject after the class does.

- **Note-Taking**

Note-taking is a controversial subject among teachers and students alike. Some students need to write to remember while others are distracted by the same activity. It is suggested note-taking be a self-chosen activity if done. Personal experience has shown that it consumes valuable time, leads to errors in writing, and even worse, often the notes are inaccurate. On the other hand, note-taking may assist the student in remembering what has been taught, depending on the accuracy of the note-taking.

To require notes to be handed in for grades is probably more a test of the student's ability in writing rather than actual knowledge gained. A better way to approach this might be what is called the OPEN OUTLINE, where the aim is to write the headings, note questions, and ideas for focus of learning, with the student filling in spaces or adding personal notes at will.

Handouts of charts, forms, or outlines can be very helpful when the facilitator is writing the key ideas on the chalk board or over-head projector, or where they are presented in PowerPoint format.

- **Structured Discussions**

Discussions that are essentially conversations between the facilitator and the students can be most helpful. Sometimes an unstructured discussion becomes the sharing of ignorance. Using well-thought-out, leading questions prompts healthy and helpful intercourse. A skilled facilitator can move the class toward the objective without losing the interest of the class.

When discussion is structured by the facilitator, control is maintained and progress toward the objective can be easily monitored and directed.

- **Performance Tryout or Simulations**

*Transferring the Vision*

Performance simulations can be highly profitable if the new learning involves a skill, such as witnessing, public speaking, or teaching. Tryouts are often necessary for evaluation and determining progress toward the objective. This can consist of a student attempting to teach a lesson in an imagined classroom setting.

- **Critiquing**

In conjunction with performance simulations or tryouts, learning to positively critique a student's performance is imperative. It not only helps the one who is trying out, but it allows the entire group to participate in evaluation and subsequent learning.

- **Role-playing**

Role-playing is similar to a tryout, but more than one person is involved. It allows the students to enact situations they have encountered or may encounter. This exercise is designed for the working out of solutions to situations rather than the actual evaluation of learning. For example, the class may be learning to conduct healthy group discussions with their problems. A group role-play can be set up to see what problems arise in a group and why. They can then seek solutions to the situations encountered. Again, critiquing or open discussion of the outcome can provide a great learning opportunity.

Each of these techniques, when practiced by the facilitator, can be beneficial to the student and the learning process. As with any skill, these or any technique must be practiced. To conduct teaching well, especially when utilizing new and untested (to the instructor) techniques, the teacher must overcome the fear of not performing well. Remember, just as with the student (who generally does not know if you have done well or not) in time and with practice any facilitator can strengthen their skills of teaching for the sake of the students and the Kingdom of God.

## Chapter 8

## Making the Class Come Alive

Up to this point what has been presented has been much theory and philosophy of education or training, but the real test comes when you begin to prepare and teach a class. Having discussed in some detail various theories and their application, we now take all the theory into consideration in planning the classroom experience. This is both an exciting and challenging opportunity.

Working with adults who have already been to school is challenging on several fronts. Naturally, adult students will, at least in their mind and expectation, tend to repeat the methods they have experienced as children in school. As a rule, we teach as we were taught in spite of all we are told.

To help the adult student to learn with positive anticipation, there are a few important things to consider.

- The instructor is challenged to create a physical climate conducive to learning. For example, it is in the best interest of adult students not to have desks in even rows, though this may seem more efficient. Desks in a row, reminiscent of elementary education, many well hinder open discussion between students, or between students and teacher. Frankly, desks are not always best, but thin writing tables are better, especially if set up where students can actually see each other as well as the instructor.

- Class arrangement must be designed so that: All students can see and interact with other students, and can easily see and interact with the facilitator. Further, it is important, as noted above, to provide (where possible) a place for students to write notes conveniently. If desks are not available, 9"x 12" writing boards may be substituted. The arrangement of the room can be varied; squares, circles, semicircles, U shaped, V s, etc. The key is to develop and maintain a non-threatening and a comfortable as possible environment, which is conducive to learning.

Along with the classroom environment, the instructor must prepare himself or herself for the actual learning process. This includes;

- Knowing why you are teaching the class, having clearly stated and understood course objectives.
- Having a clearly stated goal that you intend to attain during the specific class time.
- Knowing the students you will be working with. You cannot lead them to learn until you

know who they are, what their desires are, what goals they share, what experiences have shaped their worldview and what specific strengths and weakness they bring to the learning environment. The teacher must establish a relationship with the student to facilitate his/her learning. You will be working with individuals, not a group; you are teaching students, not subjects.
- Decisions regarding time, place, duration, breaks, and other details should be made in advance of the class and in consultation with the students where possible. The facilitator should make sure the students understand the various rules of engagement within the classroom before instruction begins.
- No matter how many times you have taught a given subject, each class has new people and it will be a new and different experience. Make it fresh by preparing your lesson well. Make sure you are able to do all of the lessons or assignments yourself to anticipate potential problems. Along with this, try to think of all the possible questions that may be asked or problems that may arise. The preparation of questions ahead of the class can help facilitate discussion and strengthen the learning process.
- Personal preparation is vital to effective teaching, and should always include much prayer. We need as much anointing to teach

as to preach. The effectiveness of our teaching will be in direct measure to the Spirit's power working through us. The Spirit will work in direct proportion to the time spent with Him.
- Lastly, make sure you personally have experienced what you are teaching to the student. The voice of experience counts.

Our primary concern in teaching is to create a spiritual and intellectual climate for learning. This is best done as we;

- Establish a bond of friendship through demonstrating genuine care for each student. Students are not names on an attendance sheet. Part of each class should be spent in building bridges of understanding. After all, this is not secular learning but spiritual life building.
- A well prepared facilitator will draw every learner into the group. Seating should be designed to stimulate interaction and minimize the natural human tendency to "get to church early to get the back seats."
- Where possible, excepting for lectures that are primarily informational only, classes of 15-20 students are ideal for discussion. People reduce their interaction in inverse proportion to the number in the group. Larger groups will

*Transferring the Vision*

be dominated by extroverts, further reducing healthy interaction.
- Be sure you know each student's name. One of the best ways to show respect for a person is to acknowledge them by name. This is an art form that professional instructors practice. Along with calling students by name, you will want to note absences, and determine the reason for such absences. Do what needs to be done to get a student back to class as soon as possible. Your showing interest in them can make a difference in a student continuing in class or dropping.
- If you have assigned work, reading, activity, or practice, check what work has been done. Ask for reports, listen to the students testimonies, by all means read the students' papers, help them correct errors, give time for questions regarding work that has been accomplished. If what they have done is not noted or recognized, it is unlikely they will take their own work seriously in the future.
- Remember, as the mentor, you are in control of what is discussed. Direct the discussion ever so deftly with questions, comments and added material. Refuse to lecture or give answers that can come from the students themselves.
- Be ready to accept questions, interruptions, comments or even interference with a loving and gentle spirit and direct students towards

the objectives. It might help to remember what my dear mother once told me. There is a reason God gave you two ears and one mouth: it is so you can listen twice as much as you talk. Good advice for today.

- Above all, keep the student at the center of your thinking, planning and facilitating, not the lesson content. Though you do want to follow the lesson plan, you are not tied to it. Teach your plan so you finish on time where possible. It is better to quit a few minutes early than a few minutes late. If a student needs or demands special attention, take time with them after the class hour.
- As a teacher, you are not in class to display your superior knowledge. You should be learning as well, as none of us have reached the full stature of the measure of Christ. Thus, if you don't know something, be humble enough to admit it and say you will find the answer. Adult students already know that you do not know everything, so why tempt them to call your bluff or despise your false front. You are not an expert, but a fellow disciple growing in the Lord.

## Conclusion and Reflection

I hope you have enjoyed learning more about learning, and the process of teaching or mentoring adults. It is my hope also that you will review these lessons often to evaluate how you are doing.

It is my prayer that the Lord will bless you as you prepare others to minister in their giftedness. As you facilitate learning, especially through the teaching of the word of God, you continue to fulfill the Great Commandment of our Lord, to make disciples of all people groups. Through teaching and facilitating learning, you will be multiplying your own ministry through your disciples just as Jesus did.

*Stan E. DeKoven, Ph.D.*

*Transferring the Vision*

*Stan E. DeKoven, Ph.D.*

www.ingramcontent.com/pod-product-compliance
Lightning Source LLC
Chambersburg PA
CBHW020019050426
42450CB00005B/541